A pretty sight
DAVID O'MEARA

Coach House Books | Toronto

first edition

 Canada Council   Conseil des Arts   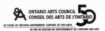 ONTARIO ARTS COUNCIL   Canadä
for the Arts   du Canada   CONSEIL DES ARTS DE L'ONTARIO

Published with the generous assistance of the Canada Council for the
Arts and the Ontario Arts Council. Coach House Books also
acknowledges the support of the Government of Canada through the
Canada Book Fund and the Government of Ontario through the
Ontario Book Publishing Tax Credit.

LIBRARY AND ARCHIVES CANADA CATALOGUING IN PUBLICATION

O'Meara, David, 1968-, author
     A pretty sight / David O'Meara.

Poems.
Issued in print and electronic formats.
ISBN 978-1-55245-281-3 (pbk.).--ISBN 978-1-77056-359-9 (epub)

     I. Title.

PS8579.M359P74 2013   C811'.54   C2013-904123-0

A *Pretty Sight* is available as an ebook: ISBN 978 1 77056 359 9.

Purchase of the print version of this book entitles you to a free digital
copy. To claim your ebook of this title, please email sales@chbooks.com
with proof of purchase or visit chbooks.com/digital. (Coach House
Books reserves the right to terminate the free digital download offer at
any time.)

for Dorothy

Spoiler Alert

Wood warps.
Glass cracks.

The whole estate
goes for a song.

The cardboard
we used

to box up the sun
didn't last long.

Contents

Occasional

As Poet Laureate of the Moon
    I'd like to welcome you
        to the opening of the Armstrong Centre

for the Performing Arts. I was asked to prepare
    a special verse to mark
        this important occasion. And I'd be the first

to confess: the assignment
    stumped me. Glancing around my workspace's
        dials and gauges, and the moonscape

through triple hermetic Plexiglas,
    I struggled to settle on the proper content
        to hard-text into the glow of my thought-screen.

In the progress of art and literature, the moon's
    been as constant a theme as rivers or the glare
        of the sun, though even after several bowls

of potent plum wine, a T'ang poet would never
    have guessed, addressing this satellite across
        the darkness, that someone would ever write back.

The Centre itself, I know, isn't much;
    a duct-lined node bolted to the laboratory,
        powered by sectional solar panels mounted

on trusses, parked not far from the first
    Apollo landing. We live with bare minimum:
        cramped, nutrient-deprived, atrophying

like versions of our perishables
    in vacuum-pack. The lack's made my sleep
        more vivid. Last night I dreamt I was in

a pool where cattle hydrated, then
    fell tenderly apart in perfect lops of meat.
        (I see a few of you nodding there in the back.)

So what good will one room do us? Maybe
    none. Maybe this streamlined aluminum
        will become our Lascaux, discovered by aliens

ages hence, pressing them to wonder what
    our rituals meant, what they said of our hopes and fears.
        Somewhere in this lunar grind, in the cratered gap

between survival and any outside meaning,
    must be the clue to our humanity, the way
        Camus once argued the trouble for Sisyphus

wasn't the endless failure to prop
    a rock atop some hill, but the thoughts
        he had on the way back down.

Which brings me to the astronauts of Apollo 11.
    After snapping the horizon through the lens
        of a single Hasselblad, knowing every boot tread

they left was eternal, they'd squeezed
    through the hatch of their landing module, shut
        and resealed it for return to Earth,

then discovered, due to cramped space
        and the bulk of their spacesuits, they'd crushed
                the switch for the ascent engine. The rockets failed

to activate. So Buzz Aldrin used part of a pen
        to trigger the damaged breaker, toggling until
                it fired the sequence for launch. This

was the quiet work of his engineer's mind.
        He kept the pen for the rest of his years,
                which is another kind of thinking, akin to *that*

slight pivoting, as Camus would call it,
        when we glance backward over our lives.
                What we keep in the pause between facts

might be the beginning of art. Which is where
        we are in this room tonight. I'll have to stop there;
                the teleprompter is flashing for wrap-up. Following

tonight's program, I'm happy to announce
        an extra ration of Natural Form and H_2O
                will be served by the airlock. I think

you're in for quite a show. So hold on
        to your flight diapers as we cue the dancers
                who've timed their performance to the backdrop

of Earthrise. There it is now in the tinted
        north viewpoint. Look at that, folks. To think
                they still find bones of dinosaurs there.

Background Noise

Home, my coat just off, the back room
murky and static, like the side altar of a church, so at first

I don't know what I hear:
one low, sustained, electronic note

keening across my ear. I spot
the stereo glow, on all morning, the CD

at rest since its final track, just empty signal now,
an electromagnetic aria of frequency backed

by the wall clock's whirr, the dryer droning in the basement,
wind, a lawn mower, the rev and hum of rush hour

pushing down the parkway. I hit the panel's power button,
pull the plug on clock and fridge, throw some switches,

trip the main breaker, position fluorescent cones to stop traffic.
Still that singing at the edge of things.

I slash overhead power lines, bleed the radiator dry,
lower flags, strangle the cat

so nothing buzzes, knocks, snaps or cries.
I lock the factories, ban mass

gatherings, building projects and roadwork,
any hobbies that require scissors, shears, knitting needles, cheers,

chopping blocks, drums or power saws. It's not enough.
I staple streets with rows of egg cartons. I close

the airports, sabotage wind farms, lobby
for cotton wool to be installed on every coast. No luck.

I build a six-metre-wide horn-shaped antenna, climb
the gantry to the control tower, and listen in.

I pick up eras of news reports, Motown, Vera Lynn, *Hockey
Night in Canada*, attempt to eliminate all interference,

pulsing heat or cooing pigeons, and yet there it is:
that bass, uniform, residual hum from all directions,

no single radio source but a resonance left over
from the beginning of the universe. Does it mean

I'm getting closer or further away? It helps to know
whether we're particle, wave or string, if time

and distance expand or circle, which is why
I need to learn to listen, even while I'm listening.

Socrates at Delium

What do I know? At least these
last two mornings since the Boeotian
ranks massed. The whole lot of us
had been camped inside their border, sea
at our backs. We thought we'd soon
be home in Athens. A set of cooking fires
still smoked behind the earthworks, evidence
of a hurried defence at the temple we'd occupied,
an obvious insult. The old seer took
the ram and made a lattice of its throat,
our counter-prayer
for the terror we hoped to inspire.
Across the dawn fields, the enemy trod
through the stripped orchards and wheat,
farmers like us, setting out cold in linen
and cloaks, the well-to-do armoured
for glory out front. After weeks of marching,
the suddenness of it: the general's shouts,
his interrupted speech passed down the lines,
our pipe marking the pace, and far off,
their war cry rending the November air
like a thousand sickles. The black doors
of each empty farmhouse watched our lines
clatter through stubbled stalks,
my arm already heavy from the shield.
'Stay tight, stay tight,' we called across
the bronze rims, cursing and half out of breath.
Then a new shout went out
and we spilled up the ridge at a run
into the Thebans' spear thrusts.

In the push, there's little room for a view;
dust scuffed up by thousands of men
gagged the air. Best to trust in detail,
watch for sharp jabs at your throat,
stay flush with the column, and above all else
don't fall. Not so easy with the friendly shields
pressing behind, and reaped furrows
snatching your balance. Our phalanx
held, shoving, and forced the Thebans
back over ground they'd claimed at midday.
But there was a too-easy feel to it,
as if we expected they'd break, and we'd slide
through their lines like lava from Hades.
Word spread of horsemen on the hill.
A trick? Who knew? We were servants
to rumour. A few turned and ran,
then the rest. Then I did too.
'Don't show them your backs,' I cried
to a group, shopkeepers from the look
of them. 'Do you want wounds *there*
when your corpse is exchanged?'
That turned them around.
We still had our swords. Scavenging cracked
spear-lengths to keep the cavalry off,
we backpedalled over corpses, boulders
and olive roots into dusk. That was two days ago.
More rumours follow us to Attica: Hippocrates
dead, how we were outnumbered,
whispers of the slaughter chittering in our ears
like broken cart wheels. Though we know the direction
home, we stall, not from plague that still strays
in its streets, but the shame of retreat.

Night, the cooking fires again.
We who are left, battered stragglers, scoop gruel
and wait for orders to seek out our dead.
Now, on the edge of the firelight, a rhapsode
recites an ancient passage, his voice recalling Troy,
the dark-beaked ships and grief for Patroclus.
We were brave enough, but couldn't hold.
What use is a story or a song?

The Afterlives of Hans and Sophie Scholl

'Allen Gewalten zum Trotz sich erhalten'
'Despite all the powers closing in, hold yourself up'

— *Goethe*

After the war, he stays underground,
still wary of the necessary
horse trades and occupying powers.

Le Monde, Die Zeit, New York
Times; Vietnam, Rwanda, Srebrenica:
years go by. In the stone arch of a busy

coffee house, Sophie is waving him over
past the billiards table, unfazed, looking
for all the world like she's just

breezed in from 1933
and there's no nightmare to come.
But the picture's all wrong, her face

unaged, and where are Alex,
Willi or Christoph?
Sophie sighs, presses

a hand against her brother's cheek.
'Hans, it's because we died.'
She describes the trial,

its forgone verdict, the bulbs
that burned all night in their cells,
the shared last cigarette

in the courtyard. Hans has turned
the details over again,
his memory tightening the blurs

like a Leica lens while the tension
in his face subsides
in the respite of knowing

at least they tried. They're even laughing,
aping the parrot shrieks
of Friesler's indignation,

gossiping over the Führer's last pose,
Hans with a finger
cocked against his temple.

They order *café viennois*.
Sophie pokes at the dollops of whip
while ordered traffic crawls

past the painted glass
of the window. The newest papers
in wooden clips

fanned across
the billiard nap. Skinhead rallies,
latest dictatorships. Hans makes

another hopeless gesture.
Did everything change, or nothing?
Coffees done, they consider the years

like doors they never entered,
as if history's just a lot
of people trying

to get from one room
to another. Outside, Hans
mounts the steps of a slowing tram.

Sophie ties her hair back
with an abalone barrette
as she turns

down Leopoldstrasse
and waves, looking for all the world
like she's going to haunt it.

Vicious
(or, On Dissent)

CHARACTERS
Socrates
Sid Vicious

SOC.

Wait, stranger! Why the rush? This place
just turns upon itself, so to leave is only a step
to hurrying back. What's the difference
if you pause and talk? Those scars
across your chest and face: did you once march
with spear and shield? I fought
at Potidaea and Delium. I'm Socrates, of Athens.

SID.

Yeah, I've heard that bit. Righteous bastard
with all the questions. I must be dead,
to run into the likes of you.

SOC.

Was it an accident? A sudden
fall from craggy heights? Or did you disturb
some starving animal in its sleep?
Who gave you those injuries?

SID.

I did.

SOC.

You?

SID.

I cut my chest with broken glass.

SOC.

And the scabs on the back of your hands,
were they not left by spear tips?

SID.

That was just a laugh with a cigarette, some game
we'd play in the Hampstead bedsit.

SOC.

What was the purpose?

SID.

It was funny. It was supposed to give
them second thoughts about trying to smack me.
Show them that anything they'd try
isn't half of what I've had already.

SOC.

Who are they who'd seek to harm you?

SID.

Suits and coppers. Punters in the audience. The fucking lot.

SOC.

What were the reasons for their enmity?

SID.

They didn't like us. We were wasters
and fuck-ups who wouldn't settle for what they
stood for: blind acceptance, apathy and moderation.

We pushed some buttons. Got kitted out in handcuffs,
leather, safety pins and razor blades. Nicked stuff.
Punch-ups. Three-chord songs with aggro-lyrics.
Style as revolt, arrogance over ability, violence
if the music failed. Like Rotten said, it's worth
going where you're least wanted,
since there's so much more to achieve.

SOC.
Were you an actor, or a rhapsode?

SID.
A what?

SOC.
A person skilled in reciting verse. Who takes the stage
at festivals with words stitched together so dramatically
that the rhythm of the music loads the crowd with feeling.
Years ago I met another rhapsode, who came from Ephesus.
I convinced him that the passion of his art passes through him
from gods into the audience; in effect he becomes possessed.
That when the beat and tone are right, frenzy builds,
and like the bacchants, he can momentarily lose his mind.

SID.
Yeah, sounds about right.

SOC.
When you look down upon the spectators
from the platform and see them weeping,
awestruck at the power of your tale, is it proof
you are a conduit between the gods
and the common crowd?

SID.

Are you taking the piss?

SOC.

What was the source of your enthusiasm?

SID.

Speed. Heroin.

SOC.

Are these some other, newer gods? What was their purpose?

SID.

Purpose, mate?

SOC.

Let me ask you this:
do you claim they brought disorder
into your minds, while still protecting you?

SID.

Yeah.

SOC.

Tell me, what is the meaning of virtue?

SID.

Fuck off.

SOC.

Remember, I was once like you, the stubborn
rube who stood against society's rules,
then was put on trial for revering new gods

and corrupting youth. I too pulled faces
at the world, and shouted down
the ruling powers. Didn't a jury find you
guilty of crimes against the state
and sentence death?

SID.
I got fixed for good before they had the chance.

SOC.
What was the vehicle of your death?

SID.
Drugs. It was the drugs, mate.

SOC.
Me, too. This was equally my fate.

SID.
Oh yeah? What did you in?

SOC.
Hemlock.

SID.
Where'd you get it?

SOC.
It's brought by ship from Crete or Asia Minor.

SID.
Must be good.

SOC.

The effect is satisfactory. Your legs feel heavy,
then retreat from feeling anything,
as if a cold blade went tickling up your thighs
to snip and trim off portions of your body
with a thousand nipping cuts. It leaves a chill,
a glaze that frosts toward your heart,
pinching off your breath. It was the punishment
they prescribed, all because I asked
too many questions and failed to compromise.
Ever since, I've been cited as an example
of how to live the good life. You see the paradox?

SID.

Listen, geezer, fuck right off. I wasn't
looking for a dialogue, just the karzy.
But if all this tripe you're laying out
is meant to serve me up as some stunned muppet
for your logic to outsmart, I've got a few words
you might need to chew on first,
since I'd hardly time to write some weepy memoir.
All that's left of who I was
are press interviews, Pistols footage
and video of me in skids, scarred and junkie-thin,
dancing to an Eddie Cochran song in the sheen
of a scuzzy mirror. When I came on the scene,
I was just naïve, then turned volatile;
they shoved me in the spotlight, stitched me up
with all the drugs and hype, then threw me to the wind.
I couldn't get my head right, and never surfaced.
Since you're so keen on painting
you and me as being two bin bags from
the same rubbish, I'll tell you what: the question

isn't virtue, but how you exercise it.
You can't know if a wheel rolls till you nudge it
down a slope. So where was all that search
for virtue's definition when the pro-Spartan Thirty
lodged their regime in your democracy's agora
and started topping the opposition?
Suddenly, you were keeping mighty quiet.
Remember Heraclitus: *ethos anthropos daimon*?
You got yours, didn't you?

SOC.
Are you suggesting I deserved to die that way?

SID.
No, mate, I'm just saying you must have seen
it coming, like I should've, coppers everywhere
and the tabloids predicting the end of the world.
Backing slogans like 'No Future,'
I had to go the distance, didn't I? Once the Pistols
imploded, I'd have been a pretty sight, in silk
and power tie, tugging a handgrip on the Tube,
counting off the platforms on the way to the office
and some thicko with a Green Day T-shirt shouting,
'Hey, weren't you Sid Vicious? Yeah, you did it
your way, looks like!' I think I see that now.
This afterlife must be the best detox going:
a clear head and all this time to wonder
what I think, now there's time to think it over.

SOC.
You speak as if the person you refer to
were someone else, a completely other soul
than the one you've left behind.

SID.

Look, I don't know. There's no fucking logic
in it, right? How can we know ourselves?
We change. We backpedal. We try again.
One of you blokes once said the soul's
an activity, not a state. That would give me hope.
That way, I could've worked through the trap
of being me forever. What a laugh.
This still isn't you or me talking anyway,
just proxies in a poem. We never got to play
our parts; you'd your man Plato spinning
yarns about how ridiculously smart
and virtuous you were, while I got Gary Oldman.
So what's one more tosser playing puppets
with his hand up our collective arse?

SOC.

So who are we?

SID.

A monkey's tea party, for all I know.
Counterweight to the comfortable
and approved. A fishbone in the throat of those
who never bothered asking
whether wealth and power were such
gasping pursuits. But what's a better way
to go than making one unholy noise
when you've got the world's ear?
You might've been an annoying prat,
but I'd back you every time, even while
you were turning blue across a mattress.
At night, I hear feedback so constant
I think I haven't dreamt it. There's

no wind here, no sky or streets,
not even a proper pisser,
and I'm with my mind all the time.

Dance

*'I was amazed to watch everyone dance. What were all those
people doing, bouncing, stuck to one another, enclosed in a box
of smoke?'*

— *Osel Hita Torres*

An older, more informed friend of mine
said, 'It's easy, step to one side
and sway, then turn to the other, like that …
Lift your arms, and for fuck's sake, don't *count*.
Snapping your fingers is okay. C'mon,
break it up a little, not once and once
and once then once to each side, you trout,
try a few moves between.
It's like a trance.'

I was terrified in junior high
as the cool kids shuffled in orderly rows
under the eyes of our teacher chaperones.
Prism shards sluiced off the mirror ball.
I escaped to the halls, toing and froing
the next hour away, the clues
dawning on me that being a teenager
was just a field test on an alien planet,
for seven years, to experiment with alcohol.

What *were* we doing, sneaking mickeys
in jean legs, risking a tab of acid,
slipping out to cars? No instructions,
no prescribed numbers of downs or yards
were set to measure our progress.

In back seats, sweat squeaky on vinyl, trying
to syringe pleasure into each other's skin,
results rarely startling or sacred, but like
meditation, a worthwhile erasure of the self.

I tried sitting in lotus position once, but kept
thinking I could use a drink. A short-term
escape from the pain we earn, these
games we play to get out of our heads.
You roam El Raval's archipelago of bars
while debating Cassavetes and Kurosawa
with some girl or boy who'll break your heart,
the hurt with street cred now, framed
in a long shot you learn to hold.

Umbrage

I'd spread the word that you're pretty slow
because you'd implied I was less than bright,
and there's one more thing I'd like to know:
are you wrong or am I right?

If a past disorder caused you trouble,
be it gastrointestinal, tooth or sinus,
if a privileged birth raised you in a bubble,
I'm afraid that's no excuse, your Highness,

for the back-stabbing habits of an asshole.
If you're really itching to put me in my place,
fine, let's drop the gloves, and like Picasso,
I'll happily rearrange your face.

And while you carve mine to a tragic mask,
we'll raise a chorus of the same old song,
since there's one more thing you'd like to ask:
were you right or was I wrong?

Drought Journal

The sky's stretched so white
noon stings, bleached
of shade. In the street,
baked chrome blinds
as a car passes with sudden
starred light, and the lawn's
a clump of stiff leaves
below the asthmatic scratchings
of the linden's crown.
Chrysanthemum heads wither
and crisp like rust; the choked
veins of perennials are edged
with brown, flattened to the stem.
Power lines buzz above curb dust.
A cyclist ticks by
beside the construction site;
men chew bread,
looking flayed and stunned
in the faint, bent shadow
of a backhoe's boom, the jackhammer
planted on the asphalt like a heroic
Soviet prop. The ballpark,
empty, roasts like the Negev,
just sand and brittle tufts
of grass, where Christ might
appear through the haze
and do a deal for one gulp
of bottled water. Sprinklers
whisking in the yards can't
stave off the parched decay,

their thimble-shallow spray
sponged dry by sun in minutes.
At 4 a.m., we wake
to the window banging back
on its hinges, and the downpour,
a day-for-night burst
of blurred white in street glow,
rain slashing down
and the dry roots slugging it back.

Terms

He stood at the front of the lecture hall,
rushed to explain the important themes
of the Twentieth-Century American Novel,

last class before midterms.
Our essays were weak; he wanted us
to get this, to sift the full impact

of the novel's plot, a book he clearly loved.
It was a quintessential early-winter day, sky
the colour of pasta water, stirred with flurries,

and the small break of Christmas before us.
The painted vents blew hot, drowsy breath.
'Now, one more thing,' he said, then talked

of the cancer they'd found, his treatments
and the chance of success. There'd be
a TA for the rest of term.

He blinked at his watch; the time was gone.
Silent, we loaded books into knapsacks.
'Good luck on the exam. Reread your notes.

And please, remember the motifs,' he said
as we poured toward the door,
'of the white horse and the pillar of smoke.'

Hare

Time sawing its hinds,
it crests the pasture's rump,
countless long-jumps
in a row, a pelted arrow
fletched for lift.

It shakes off *sleek* and *quick*
as too flat; its stride taps the course,
a triple-time tattoo through sprays
of heather and gorse,
where it winks, framed in haze.

Though it's said to pound
rice cakes on the moon,
a trickster or Aesop's fool,
it refuses to be other than real
when you see it running. Pity
it can't sing while the hound bears
down with that boggle-eyed stare
chugging the void
on a whisk of gangly limbs
to muzzle all zags and hearsay.

What would it sing? Psalm,
plainsong, tin pans,
cable in a squall,
cymbal crash, cackle, drag
on a rutted brake pad,
chanson to sum up our fable
before its raw chords are shot,
before its shot chords are ash.

Memento Mori

Before I am called into dinner,
    you call out, 'Come here,
come look,' lifting a cracked wand
    of bone from the dry manure

you turn in your hand
    and weigh. Kicking around,
we hunt for more parts of the set,
    limbs or rib slats fanned

out like smashed bracelets
    mislaid in the clover.
'Let's go,' I say, 'it's late.'
    You turn the thing over and over.

Circa Now
(Rhapsody)

Likely we'll have no language
    to resemble the ones we use now
        when the LAGEOS satellite finally drops

to Earth. Silver, with a solid
    brass core, its arc set
        to track our planetary shift

until its highly stable orbit
    deteriorates in the year 8,000,000.
        Any sense of its first purpose

will be lost to whoever
    might still be here. What they'd
        look like, eat or dream is anyone's

guess, but we fixed a plaque inside
    with drawings of the Earth, circa now,
        and another one with future coastlines

fanned out like a stretched accordion
    to show them how the world might look
        after 80,000 inches of continental drift,

one every century. If anything's left
    to inspect those shifted silhouettes –
        our prodigal land mounted in a dimpled,

silver ball – they might just
      read them as portent, threat or tall saga
          cooked up by a far-too-distant race

to understand.

•

In Fort Kochi, Kerala,
a long day of walking the baked stretch
of Bazaar Road past the ferry terminal
to Ernakulam. Textiles, pots, oils, ceramics,
paper and tobacco spilled for sale
from the open shutters of the shops.
Goats nudged garbage while the touts
called out to *please look*
at their leather sandals, sarongs
and elephant tea cozies. The dance
of haggling, offers
and countered head shakes.
Mosquitoes devoured your bare legs
under the batik tablecloth
as we sat for biryani and curry.
I'd spread the newspaper out,
looking for news of home
in a tiny font. But read
a report of the Italian snail
thriving on the grounds
at Cliveden and a theory about
how it got there: stowaway in 1896
on a marble balustrade
imported from the Villa Borghese.

Structures of one empire humped
across shipping lanes to another,
the marvel of Rome raided for newer money,
while the snail
plods its slime trail
twenty-seven metres each century.

•

For those who cite *The Matrix*, *Rocky*
　　and the CGI'd prequels to *Star Wars*
　　　　as good reason to hate them,

remember the *Aeneid* is also a sequel.
　　And remember a thousand years
　　　　separate Homer and Virgil, only

two thousand more between Virgil
　　and us. War that follows rage, the care
　　　　of fields and horses, some details might

still ring so true that he seems
　　near each time we hear them.
　　　　Hungry, Virgil crosses the bridge

to Trastevere, adjusts his toga
　　beside a line of smart cars, catching
　　　　the whiff of dinner venting through

trattorie shutters. In a doorway,
　　he watches the chef bent over
　　　　a scratched counter, who steadies

then chops an onion's soft, rotten
        underside until he frees crisp layers
                lambent at its core, sautés them

in olive oil with garlic,
        the sizzle and smell
                so familiar the poet might forget

Maecenas isn't waiting to debate
        rhetoric or Aeneas's fate
                in the gardens up the Esquiline Hill.

                •

Where does the Danube start?
Magris searches in his book.
He visits Furtwangen

with friends, finds a brook
that drains into a tributary,
the exact source

an argument for centuries, inch
by sodden inch. Near a clear spring
on a hill, they reach a dip

rinsed with rivulets,
and follow a slope to a house
where they knock

at the threshold, squint into a window.
Feet shuffle through half-empty rooms
to the door

which opens on a perturbed old woman
not interested in questions.
But since they've

come all this way, she listens, squints
and points to a rough ditch near
a woodshed

gushing cold water. 'The water reaches
the gutter,' she explains,
'through a basin,

which is constantly full because of a tap
that no one ever succeeds
in turning off.'

•

I never tire of arriving.
At Pamukkale, the wind chucked
leaves and palm fronds as we crossed
the main square.
Barefoot, we ascended
the travertine rock, its stalactites' drip
and slow froth of calcium
like an overpoured pint of Guinness
cooled to dollops of white-rimmed shelves.
Ruins at the top,
the once-bustling spa town of Heirapolis,
its paving stones still rutted
by the wear of cart wheels.
Here you can walk past the colonnades
of antiquity's shops. Wealthy Romans

took the hot springs here, retired
and died, their sarcophagi
accumulating to another kind
of stop for tourists north of the baths.
Shells of modern tourism too, lobby fragments
from the 1970s, more evidence of
how eras settle, retreat,
each strata engraved as ghost structure.
This abandoned front desk, the green
marble floor at dusk, light like soft copper,
haunting as any wheel rut
crowded with weeds –
you can find them if you follow
these unmarked goat tracks
further still.

•

'If I cannot bend the higher powers,
I will move the infernal regions.'

A favourite quote of Freud's
and the Secessionist painters of Vienna,

lovers of the glimpse, the held-back, what
beats at your insides to claw a way out.

I wrote it down looking at Klimt's *Attersee*
in the Leopold Museum south of the Ringstrasse.

The words are Juno's in Virgil's *Aeneid*,
a summation of alternative options

for those cast outside the party line.
The ode to Plan B.

Attersee might be landscape
as subversive frill,

the lake's abstract surface
stroked with turquoise

over green and blue underpaint
like the bangled skies of Van Gogh.

Klimt's lake
stretches, infinitely if it could,

to the top edge of canvas
and the dark, heavy shape painted there,

an island or shoreline that by limiting
the infinite has given it value.

•

I thought I saw Sophie Scholl
in a club underground

in Warsaw
that we found by following smokers

down an alley and steep, concrete stairwell,
through tobacco fog to air-sucking bass.

She was nodding at the mosh edge,
beer clutched in her hand

in that post–Cold War dance hall.
I wanted to ask how she got there –

roaming the rebuilt
squares of *Mitteleuropa* – but she looked

too happy to bother
with dredging up the past. Anyway, what

would be the question?
Is everything changed, or the same?

knowing any answer won't change
the hour of closing time. In that basement's low ceiling

and sticky floor, furnished
in the dumpster vogue

of old fridges and mismatched chairs,
Sophie hardly blinked, swigged

her drink, her silence meant
as challenge to 'put up or shut up'

or just 'shut up and listen.'
In the speakers' blare

I left her there.

•

We were returning from the north,
an overnight train
from Sa Pa, sharing a sleeping berth
with two young women from Switzerland.
It was 4 a.m. as the rubbed glow
of the station platform settled in our window.
We lugged backpacks
through the puzzle of Hanoi's Old Quarter,
amazed at its paused frenzy, dark shops
locked behind metal gates, a few motorbikes
chainsawing past. A cafe opened at 5:30
and agreed to hold our packs
so we wandered to Hoan Kiem Lake
to watch the tai chi groups
balance inner tensions at sunrise.
By then, completely transformed,
the market and streets were stacked
with baskets: crab, pork,
pineapple pyramids, oysters
and sleek trout hawked by vendors,
attendants sweeping park paths
with long, wiry brooms. Police brewed tea
in their dawn kiosk, caps
angled back
off their foreheads
near stereos wired to trees
for the tai chi grannies, conjuring
longevity with techno beats.
Hanoi's traffic and street life,
no history but the deal, offers
and banter, the good price of fish
caught that morning

in the Gulf of Tonkin.
Fuck silence or permanence.
Fuck elegy. Fuck time and pain.

·

Dawn sky, sriracha red,
Chiang Mai lunch, khao soi and mango,
a stockpile of sun before
another carousel of departure level,
the sucker-punch intake of takeoff.
Past weightless snatches of sleep,
the drop
to the terminal bus, that sub-zero palanquin
aloft over road drifts
of Baltic night:
watch as we hurried through snowfall
to brew tea and read in the lamplight
of a Helsinki hostel.

·

Olduvai, really *Oldupai*,
        named for the fronded sisal plant
                that grows here. Seen from space,

the Rift's a patchwork
        in algal patina, the gorge
                a grey-green collage splayed

with evaporated rill beds,
        steep cracks tracking the landscape
                like plate sutures on a skull. Snacking

on sandwiches, we sat under
    corrugated tin, protected
        from the sun's hazy weight,

rock monolith and broken scrub
    hedging the Earth's curvature.
        Three and a half million years back,

three apes, predate of humans,
    walked past at Laetoli through drops
        of soft rain, the shapes of their prints

left by the ash layer, cemented
    in tuff, stable enough to last
        as the hot and grey ash fell.

Other marks: birds, a hare,
    a three-toed horse
        and its foal turning

in the opposite
    direction. Dimpling the site,
        rainprints too. But this trio, tracks

tagged 61, 62 and 63,
    we know walked upright, as a habit;
        left no knuckle marks, the gait

a 'small-town walking speed'
    like a stroll through the agora.
        Tempting to speculate

about the story of their travel,
    a family or hunting group
        looking for signs of a water hole

in the wake of the volcano's
    tremors, one set of their prints
        nested in the hollow of another,

the way we can follow
    someone through snow
        to make the going a little easier.

•

On a charity box in the Hanoi airport:
'For Especially Difficult Children.'
Or 'We Beg for Silent Behaving' outside
the Basilica of St. Euphemia
in Rovinj, Croatia.
I mention this not from smugness
but as point of argument. If language blurs
across cultures in the same decade,
how will our songs and stories
translate across ticking inches of drift?
The challenge of Onkalo,
'hiding place,' a toxic dump
cored through granite in Finland.
Blasters descend through rock
five kilometres deep,
bore igneous strata, each layer
another geologic age.
So when they drive

their pickups down and walk
through curtains of dust, are
they descending back through time
in corridors designed to be resealed
and forgotten for a thousand centuries?
How silent it will be, down
there, when the ventilation fans
stop whirring,
the new Ice Age crested
and gone, Earth's surface scoured
like a child's ribboned aggie found
in the grass near a gravel road.
We'll have no language
to warn of what we built, no marker
left to explain the world
wiped clear of any signs of us.
'My bones would rest much easier,'
Virgil wrote, 'if I knew your songs
would tell my story in days to come.'

·

Let me be quieter. Go

slow and listen.
        Near Lake Manyara,
                the unhurried swish

of elephants
        gnashing through branches
                as we sat for an hour

49

just watching. Ibises rested
in the umbrella acacias,
velvet monkeys

in the grass. Remember
the Ngorongoro Crater?
We stood on its rim

past dusk; uninterrupted herds
of wildebeest and zebra
migrating below

the distant lightning storm.
Go slow, I thought. *Listen.*
That morning, as we left

Arusha, our truck passed
a group of Masai
headed to town.

'How do they get around?'
'They walk. They'll walk
to Nairobi. You can't

walk like the Masai.'
The warriors leaned
on their spears, waiting

to cross the red dirt
of the Serengeti road.
Easy to imagine

their indifferent looks
    as pre-Homeric,
        outwaiting time

with a cubist view,
    so looking out
        is always looking in,

so wherever you turn,
    you arrive just
        as you're leaving,

though I knew
    a likely goal in town
        might be the internet,

or to change
    from dyed *shuka*
        to tailored suits

and a government posting.

       •

At the check-in counter at Heathrow,
I took a snap of our backpacks.

Who knows what we really need?
Baggage for some estate lawyer

to inventory, and meanwhile we're carried
like stowaway snails on shipped marble

through Earth's shallow atmosphere,
that dark shape near the edge of the canvas.

•

Virgil, don't be our guide; you wouldn't
know the way around now.
Wandering below the Palatine
in hopes of a dinner invitation,
you'd need to pause at every turn
between fountains, churches,
papal scavenging
or Domitian's renos further on.
The Christ thing? Long story;
born nineteen years after you died,
he changed the architecture, to put
it mildly. That's just the start.
Since I'm buying lunch, let's stop at one
of these pizza counters that line
the tourist route and I'll explain
coffee, tomatoes and pasta to you.
Here's the Pantheon, its columns and porch
propped on the sudden rotunda.
You know the site as Agrippa's temple,
gone now, yes, but step inside,
they've done wonders.
Marvel at the symmetric swirl
of its ceiling tiles, the open dome
tipping light and rain across the stone.
Hey, I know a good fish place
not far from here, just down
from the Campo de' Fiori, that serves

battered cod and antipasti
with a decent jug of *vino sfuso*.
Nothing fancy. A lino floor, white linen
thrown across a few rough tables; the waiters
Old World Romans who rush
to shake your hand at the exit.
It's around here, I swear, somewhere,
though it's been a couple of years
and you never know
how business will go, I don't need
to tell you. All that's fallen or torn down
evades our partial gaze
yet ruins still wait to brush against us
from the afternoons they were raised.
If you've asked us to wait
by this intersection, it must be the feel
of something familiar, a turn
in the street where the plastered
porticoes of *insulae* once stood.
You could close your eyes, cued by pigeon trills,
and hear the cart wheels on basalt,
or smell the reek of garum
before engines interrupt, and cellphones.
Contrails rib the sky.

'In Event of Moon Disaster'

– William Safire (July 1969)

After Borman,
NASA's liaison, calls
and urges 'some alternative posture'

should things go south – unforeseen glitch,
miscalculation,
technical whatever – leaving

Armstrong and Aldrin
stranded on the moon,
does Safire walk or run

to the Oval Office?
The president's aides rustle
around the furniture, their minds

touchy and tentative
like bees
in a cactus patch.

You can imagine Dick's face
when advised: cut all
communication, commend

their souls to 'the deepest
of the deep,' like a burial at sea.
Then call their wives.

As for text, it's left
to Safire
to get the spirit right. Christ,

this will be either
the speech of his life or words
that are never uttered.

Though he's no pacer, there
he goes on Penn Ave., ditching
the ride to a deli

with the government driver,
insisting he'll take
the few last blocks on foot.

He wants the air
of a summer night and an uncluttered sense
of the quotidian.

The stars might pull at time
like taffy out there, exhaling light,
but it's reassuring to know

that in the suburbs
someone's washing dishes, a curtain
is lifted by the breeze

and surely there's a midget team
looking for a homer under bug-infested
ballpark lights.

At the meat counter, he watches
them shave a sheaf
of pastrami onto the waxed sheet, pop

bread and mini packs
of mustard into paper sacks,
provisions

for what's going to be
an all-nighter in a toe-to-toe
with the typewriter.

If only he could peel
back the top of his head
to reveal slick words laid neatly

and glistening like that
cache of silver found
when a sardine key gets twisted round.

But all he can see
are two dead astronauts
canned in welded metal,

their ingress above the module's ladder
like Jacob's climb to heaven
and everything a question of how

anyone would spend their last few hours.
Would *you* stay inside, waiting till
the oxygen goes critical, tapping

the dead switch for the ascent engine
in a lonely Morse? Or, rather,
pull an Oates, and wander out into the cold

for one last stroll,
the whirling white like tickertape.
Safire slows

at the thought of it. All night
he'll haunt his office, taunted
by shades of scenario,

the moon's milky glow
hung in its pure potential,
stalled like those satellites of paper

balled up into the waste,
the future an empty shape
still left to fill with explanation.

In Kosovo

Berna, whose friends call her Bass Face,
looks more like a sylph with a grudge.
Her head, half-shaved and delicate, stares
and unsettles you while a fat beat drubs

through her ad hoc PA. She owns
this club, one of the few with decent sound
in war-scarred Pristina.
As the latest power cut ends,

ravers drift back to the dance floor
while a drum 'n' bass rumble is laid down
over Springsteen's 'Dancing in the Dark.'
No pop snobs, they'll shout and pump hands

at the first moaning notes, as the DJ
digs in to beat-mix a long set
of minimal techno, dubstep and house.
He doesn't scratch; this is *way*

post-Detroit. It's fucking Kosovo, 2008;
even the potholes have potholes.
Air strikes from NATO sent Slobodan
packing, but left each street

with a trail of bomb damage, blackouts
and overtaxed hospitals. Call that history;
I'm sure the kids would love to give
a shit, but just now they're too busy dancing,

each beat a real rush, every move a one-fingered
salute to the past. The trance scene's across town,
but all the DJs mix with a shared set of decks.
There's Legoff, Toton, Goya and Likatek.
And Berna, whose friends call her Bass Face.

Ten Years

> – another for Andrea Skillen

Your massive metallic sports watch
bristled like a gunship,
so wearing it was your mutinous raspberry
to the elegant dress, necklace
and ring they were burying you in.
Your brother confided you'd set the alarm
but hadn't said for when.
It was perfectly grand and inappropriate,
an antidote to the bathetic pageant
we'd kitted ourselves into with awkward suits
across the solemn tones
of the parlour's coloured carpet.

This morning I've been listening
to some Buffalo Tom and 'the Man in Black,'
calling back the summer
we hung in hope for you,
the autumn, the winter, the spring ...
I housesat all your things, most in boxes
for the move to Winnipeg you never made,
a lease you had to break, those vacant rooms
still waiting like Virgil's version
of the Cumaean Sibyl's cave,
her prophecies writ on oak leaves
and kept in order, unless some mortal
should open the door and scatter them.

The Tennis Courts in Winter

From Christmas through the end of March
I'd been trying to find some clever way to start
a poem called 'The Tennis Courts in Winter.'
I passed them every day on my snowbound lurch
up Delaware and Cartier, the east-side court
still posting rules of play, the stiffened board off-kilter

where the zip ties snapped. But every chance
I'd get to jot the title down was stopped by white below.
My unwritten poem had become the tennis courts,
frozen to a stop inside a chain-link fence,
blocked and blank, the obliterating snow
like revelation in reverse, which, of course,

is just forgetting. But I don't forget, and don't know why
the title haunts me; it might have something to do
with potential. Yesterday I thought of it again,
though it's been years since I moved away
to this other neighbourhood and the snow
has come and gone at least a hundred times since then.

So Far, So Stupid

All those selfies I posted
look really great. So spontaneous. Arm

tentacled through bad light past the frame,
an umbilical toward my ego.

Freud, meet Descartes. Intentions,
like airports, look deceptively the same,

then you get a security pass
for the doors just off the escalators.

Inside my mind, there's another mind,
like a prop warehouse,

dramatically cluttered at times.
I go there, for the wind machine

and free-standing door
I just slam and slam.

Somewhere, Nowhere

There was little time left to be young
and stupid, so I hitched due west
on the 17, cold thumb to autumn.
Outside Sault Ste. Marie, ground mist
and the turned-up collar.
I slept in a ditch.

A man from Provence waved
me toward a camper van; we traded
goals of getting to the coast,
though he talked of Fresno,
Oaxaca, and the way south to Chile.

North of Superior, the going
was rough on gear and brake, flashes
of lake between terraces of the Seven's
granite and pine. Past dark,

we found a side road, parked, ate
sandwiches, bet almonds on cards,
talked origins of Mad Hatter
and Winnie the Pooh. Inside
my sleeping bag, with no bleed
from the usual streetlights,
it was an inkwell cave.

It was medieval night
and I ceased feeling any links
to what was real, just a stinging
trust at being in the middle of nothing

but my life. It was like that for days,
until I was dropped off near Golden,
the boot knife velcroed to my ankle,
symbol of how luck and stupidity
ride the same edge.

No One

No one knows what's going on
in your head; we just watch
the slow stir behind your eyes
like granola through yogourt.
Outside the clubs we spilled from, taxis
ushered us from our shame
to fraught mornings we'll have to own
for all the good they do.
And I still haven't heard from you.
You're not nowhere. You've eaten
the crumbs of some trail.
Odd jobs and broken homes
deflate us. The air isn't all gone,
though we sag with our lies
like used mattresses. And anything
improves but not without effort.
Horseshit doesn't just turn into pizza.
You've stopped answering doors,
disappear further behind DVDs
and baseball stats. Like you,
I'm no natural, but I hold on with
dumb hope I might poke one
out of the infield on a funny bounce.
Our trust is more than shaken,
though we've been through the wars,
the nights, the birthdays.
I'm grateful, it's true,
and no one can speak for you.

Reclining Figures

'... you must experiment. You do things in which you eliminate
something which is, perhaps, essential — but to learn how
essential it is, you leave it out.'

— Henry Moore

1 Michelangelo, *Night* (1526–31)

She still lolls, propped on the pediment
of the Medici tomb in Florence.
Her right elbow rests on a thick left thigh
that twists from the edge, half-aware
she must stay balanced there.
She's tired. Is she catching some shut-eye
so she'll stay fresh and be admired
for the next five hundred years? Stare
at the braided clump of hair that drops
across a breast, the white stomach
like stepped folds of sand left by the tide.
Has flesh ever been more alive
than in this marble? We touch a hand
against her neck; she starts and lifts her eyes.

2 Moore, UNESCO, *Reclining Figure* (LH 416, 1957–58)

        Its sea-stack
        vertical tatter. Dry rills
and dints squirrelled themselves
from worked boulder –
        into shoulders, hips, elbows – a shape
        hurrying to the surface
only once the mind has turned
and turned to find it.
        The loosely
        knotted sign for the self
ghosted from a stab
        at what he guessed
        might show itself, form
or the starving aperture at its centre.

3 Moore, *Reclining Figure* (LH608, 1969–70)

A phone call from my buddy
one night in Southend
about some work
that might be worth a few.

We rolled up to this estate
past midnight, in a stolen
Mercedes flatbed – some kind of museum,
barns in a dark farmyard,

and right there in the field
this blob of bronze
we had to hoist with a fucking crane,
tuck beneath a tarp,

then speed away, not exactly
clean, our labours saved
for Interpol and Scotland Yard
on CCTV.

Three of us, unlikely
to sell it intact, drove
out to a lock-up
of this scrap man, and cut

the lot up for easy passage
through Her Majesty's ports
to Rotterdam. Eight hundred
each, tax free.

A drop of it might be
in your cellphone,
'cause they shipped it on to China
and melted down

all that it's accrued
from what its *meaning is*
and what it *gestures to*
for something clearly useful.

4 Michelangelo, *Rondanini Pietà* (1552–1564?)

Moore liked best
what wasn't finished, no
'happy fixed finality.'
He eventually found *Night*'s skin
thick, too leathery and polished.
Instead, he feted the pitted heads
of Michelangelo's failed, last Pietà,
its original stonework torn
down like an expensive set of drapes
to show thinner, exhausted
shapes inside. Not Renaissance
but Gothic, more solitary
than his greatest forms, Christ's nose
and mouth chiselled flat,
Mary's supporting hand
a broken edge of marble
as if the sculptor had run out
of material space to describe their pain
so left them there to rest.
A *great question*, Moore claimed
of the Master's failures:
*they taught me what happened
in his mind*, the ideal
and its fracture both
scratching for the light.

Loot

Mushin Hasan, head in hands, is tableau
     on the cuneiform tablet. He saw it coming. How
     could he not, counting off the precedents,
from the Elamite sack of Babylon,

     umpteen sacks of Rome – Visigoth,
Saracen, Norman – to all that stuff
carted back for an empire's
     display cases, Lord Elgin

or Napoleon. What's been left alone?
     Like Layard outside Mosul, camped near villages
     the locals built on grass mounds,
their houses framed by giant stones

     inscribed with script
turned out were the walls of Nineveh.
Clay tablets from the Gilgamesh saga
     shipped up the Thames,

the Ishtar Gate to Berlin. Power
     on display as the power to take and then curate
     into ownership. More subtle than just
charging past the coat check

     with axes and iron pipes,
screaming *there is no government or state*,
but the same result.
     FOX TV loops

of looters make us forget how families
        were squeezed between a no-win/no-win
        of the home regime, overseas' sanctions
and systematic deployment

        of Tomahawk missiles.
Among computers, ACS and chairs
stripped from storerooms are plates
        from the royal tombs

of Ur, and a headless limestone figure
        chiselled in Lagash 4,400 years ago.
        Nearby, soldiers told to hold
a traffic control point, wait

        on a news crew
to get the best side of a tank-round
whacking the statue of Saddam
        on horseback. No montage

of Donny George and museum staff
        chaining the museum's front doors, taking shifts with clubs
        against gangs organized in supply chains
for the profit of foreign

        collectors. Only days
after Baghdad's invasion, fresh artefacts
surface on the Parisian
        black market. The top three

metres of southern Iraq now pockmarked,
        ransacked past dark to the clatter
        of generators and shovels. What we had
of the unexcavated sites of Adab,

        Zabalam, Umma and Shuruppak
are now empty spaces in human narrative.
The stone head of King Sanatruq,
        2nd century CE,

recovered by luck when an Italian archaeologist
        told police he'd spotted it on a mantelpiece
        of an Al Jazeera decorating show.
If my family were starving, I'd rifle

        through the storerooms.
Coalition forces pour a fresh helipad,
Chinook rotors blast sand and rattle
        the remaining walls

of ancient Babylon. The Temple of Ninmah's
        roof collapses, the halls of the Temple of Nabu.
        War's aftermath: no power, no water, no work.
So what good is art?

        Near the city's edge,
a crowd in dishdashas wears stethoscopes,
dragging around OR gear
        lifted from the hospital.

What is 'preserving the past'? Bread flour
        bakes in dried mud, near corpses from sectarian
        killings. One man, a shoe repairman,
digs up an artefact, solid gold,

        of a cow, so sells it
for a silver BMW. Every day soldiers come
to have their pictures
        taken from the top

of the bullet-notched ziggurat, each click
        an exhibit of the *I was here*, desert cam
        lost in silhouette against the level,
ochre panorama of sand.

Impagliato

(Albrecht Dürer's Rhinoceros *briefly addresses the tiger shark from Damien Hirst's* The Physical Impossibility of Death in the Mind of Someone Living*)*

I've been trying to get you
out of my mind, a rival to the crown
as art's most iconic
image of an animal.

With a half-millennium
head start, I've preened on countless
woodcut prints, a cathedral door in Pisa,
a Medici emblem,

and still am featured on tourist T-shirts,
my splayed, unlikely toes
outside the British Museum.
It's the same way

you've got presence, kid,
loitering in that cabinet,
injected with 5 percent formaldehyde,
your serrated grin

trademark to an appetite so wide
you're nicknamed *trash can*
of the ocean for gulping tires,
oil-drum lids and licence plates.

Hirst raised such a royal fuss.
Outrage hooked the media as neat
as the gaff that hooked you
off Australia, cultural status landed

by all that commission money.
Dürer never saw a real rhino;
I'm his vision of one they lost
en route to Rome

as a showpiece in the pope's menagerie.
A storm sucked the ship down,
the trapped beast
shackled to the deck.

The artist played the facts a little
fast and loose, sketched my hide
in absentia with scales and plates,
mounted a stunted horn

on my riveted nape
like a hairy twist of ice cream.
Hardly accurate, but it shocked the crowd,
half the battle in making a name.

I guess raw profit's why
the master from Nuremburg
wrought a woodcut,
not a painting, guessing sales

from copies wouldn't be outcharted
until the advent of Farrah
Fawcett. And to compensate
for investors' losses

when the carcass washed up
against the Ligurian coast,
they put it on display
'stuffed with straw.'

Talk

I thought I'd see you at one
of the shows this summer. If so,
talk might have gone in a million
directions, and been awkward, as we'd likely
keep it small, complaining of the lineups
at the beer tent, then finding
a break in the crowd to slip away.

Talk was never our problem;
all those late-night think-tanks
after closing the bar, cooking up
subtleties on invented games,
rules to 'Quick Drinks'
or 'Etch-a-Sketch Portraits.'
Though most talk was art – what might
be good and where to find it –
while we watched the floor dry,
squashed in the booth
with the lights turned low.

I know you,
so was less and less surprised
when you sidestepped
issues people tried to raise,
and worse, twisted them
into betrayal by your stubborn,
bottled-up imagination. They
were trying to show they cared
even while you bulldozed into rooms,
grim as a defeated army.

Meanwhile, work is work,
late home, five hours sleep,
coffee, then a nap. You've missed
a birth or two, the filled and emptied diapers
of friends' burping offspring,
and I've moved, so if you ever
picture me, I don't know where.
Mostly, when I think of you, I see
you angry and mistaken.
Almost daily, I bike past
your old studio
and the re-rented house,
rooms where our unsuspecting ghosts
still drink and smoke, contra Yeats,
imperfect on every count.

Silkworms

Home-grown for extra income,
they're warmed in the watts
of a standard light bulb
till the egg forms a worm, *small
like a hair*. Each one feasts
on mulberry, a month-long course
of shiny leaves, chubbing themselves
into a pale, lazy wiggle.

They wish to be a kimono cloud,
ball of fog, white
shrouds spun for their own ghosts
as they nod off to a creaking dream
of legs and wings. They wish
they were metaphor.

To let them stretch would tear
sleek work, so each cocoon
is dropped in a rolling boil, their
lives pinched out like fingers
on a match head.
The strands are reeled on a row
of spools,
and the cocoons jig and iridesce
until the corpse is undressed.

'There's Where the American Helicopters Landed'

Sixtyish, wrinkled, Ling Quang's hard look
lifts from the gravel where we've stopped,
the Honda's kickstand staked
to the road's thin shoulder,
our helmets laid like eggs on the leather seat.
He points at the place
near the silk factory where
the craters are almost overgrown,
green tangles scanned
through his knock-off Ray-Bans.

On the bike, I forget to lean
through curves, tires
eating the steep grade back to town,
past the bridge again
where a man stands fishing,
nylon net like a smudge of mist
that skims his catch from the creek,
their fins struggling in the killing air.

End Times

In the tangled field, our boots catch.
Barns wedged in thick weeds
are beached container ships
wrought in rusted brick, dust, rot whiff
of hay bales. A black stork
rigs straw on a transmission post
that sags with dead wire.
A wolf curls on a park bench,
sneers through cleft lips.
There's a trace of skew
in the oak leaves' lost symmetry.
The pond is hummingbird green.

.

The car's waved through; a triangle
signs the split where we yield
to nothing but silence. On the bridge,
corroded guardrails
fence the phantom view
of burning graphite.
Eleven flagpoles spoke
the drive at the only hotel.
The air rings, metal
lashed by slack chains.
Pine and spruce glut the playground,
split the ball court, sprout roots
in lobbies and rooftop gravel.
School floorboards
warp and rake. The pool

fills with ceiling tiles
and flaking paint.

•

There are many of us here. A whole street.
They went off just as they were, in their shirt sleeves.
Around it, burdock, stinging-nettle, and goose-foot.

I'm not supposed to be talking about this.

Everywhere we used shovels.
Get rid of the topsoil to the depth of one spade.
Changing our masks up to thirty times a shift.

I would see roes and wild boars. They were thin and sleepy,
like they were moving in slow motion.

Something glistened.
It came off in layers – as white film ... the colour of his face.
There it was – and there it wasn't.
Safer than samovars.

What we saw.
The wind blows the dust from one field to the next.
Dresses, boots, chairs, harmonicas, sewing machines. We buried it
in ditches. Houses and trees, we buried everything.
There lie thousands of dogs, cats, horses, that were shot. And not
a single name. What remains of ancient Greece?
The myths of ancient Greece.

On the one hand, it's disgusting, and on the other hand – why don't you
all go fuck yourselves?

We heard that something had happened somewhere.
So you can picture it: a lead vest, masks, the wheelbarrows
and insane speed.
The ants are crawling along the tree branch.
'In several generations'
'Forever'
'Nothing'

They brought me the urn. I felt around with my hand,
and there was something tiny, like seashells in the sand,
those were his hip bones.

Everyone became what he really was.
'Walking ashes.'

When I got here, the birds were in their nests, and when I left
the apples were lying in the snow.
That was the worst. All around, it was just beautiful.
I would never see such people again. Everyone's faces
just looked crazy. Their faces did, and so did ours.

We buried the forest.
We buried the earth.
We sawed the trees into meter-and-a-half pieces
and packed them in cellophane and threw them into graves.

They stood in the black dust, talking, breathing, wondering at it.
You can imagine how much philosophy there was.

I felt like I was recording the future.
We're its victims, but also its priests.

When I die, sell the car and the spare tire, and don't marry Tolik.

You should come into this world on your tiptoes, and stop at the entrance.
This person will be happy just to find one human footprint.

•

There's a fecund smell,
grenadine sweet,
remnants of mutant hemlock,
chestnut and wildflowers,
or it could be
cotton candy.
The Fun Fair rusts.
Stark as a double helix
of DNA, unused scaffolds
of the Tilt-A-Whirl
lean and shriek
in the refrigerated calm.

•

I don't know what I should talk about —

A ruined building, a field of debris;

I'll remember everything for you.

Sing Song

One day all those kittens and pups
we drowned in a sack
will come crawling back.
They'll drag up shit

from L.A. to the Moscow underground.
They'll claw through our exhaust,
oil and grease
that's decanted into sewer grates

by generations of squeegee kids.
Their scratches will resound
like some turntablist's retro stack
that *doo-langs*

as it's tipped from a milk crate.
They won't be fucking around.
They'll hunt us down.
They'll get a fix and calibrate

like the Hubble's squint staring in,
one eye a plaster cast
from Pompeii, the other in decay
like Chernobyl.

They'll raise a din,
their yips like drone strikes, their howls
a martyr's mother on cnn,
their meows the opinionated crap

we generated in chatrooms
so easily after the fact. Just you wait.
They're no Mutt and Jeff.
On their tags there's wto and imf

engraved in gold. And when we're found
on the business end of their gps,
they'll say, 'Did you really think
you'd give our sins the slip

by filling up some burlap
and tipping us in the drink?'
They're coming around, crammed
up the yingyang

with talking points and spreadsheets
on every bailout,
g8 summit, profit bonus
and offshore bank we ever had.

Doo-lang, doo-lang.

How I Wrote

You must change your life, but first,
wait a few minutes. After all, Rilke couch-surfed
from castle to château for a decade before
his internal mood ring shifted to purple
and signalled the muse. He finessed this later
as creative possession: an impulse so focused
he's said to forget the time of day,
though Wikipedia claims he never missed
a meal at Duino. Big deal. Whatever
it was, he could direct the spirit's surges
and knew how to work a crowd in its wake.
Imagine him on Facebook. LOL.
Precious, yes, but how not to be
when you're born in Prague and write
about angels. In any case, you won't catch me
mooning along parapets and sea walls;
not because I wouldn't, but so far
there've been no offers. I booked a week
at Banff in a forest studio,
ate scones, startled a ground squirrel,
kept forgetting to bring a jacket,
and one night heard blues harmonica
drift from the aboriginal arts lodge nearby.
I texted a friend who's Ojibwa. WTF?
He wrote back 'Why don't you go
over there and ask them what they've got
to be blue about?' Touché.
So I managed some edits, and through
the skylight watched yellow leaves
parachute the branched heights to amass

as ground cover. No thought-fox
raised its rusty snout, or gifted prints
across the page, though a few fingers
of cask-strength Scotch made
the waiting a little easier. Paradox:
to be perfectly here, you must
stop thinking about it, then it's on.
Most days I leaf around trying to sidle
out of the peripheral sight of myself,
so when I focus again, I might
be astonished, do something real, feel
like Jarrett at Köln, overtired
and saddled with the wrong piano,
forced to work the corners we get
backed into. It might be a thunderbolt,
but mostly a mule I keep thinking of
when I picture myself in the grind between
the start of some work and its end result,
but like an apprentice before the koan,
I'm afflicted by the absent revelation,
never sure if it's better to change the light bulb
or stare into the dark.

Memento Mori

A mariachi band has just begun;
the *cantinero* muddles lime, ice and mint.
Is it industry, folly or perverse fun
to lounge here, behind my glasses' darkly tint,
reading elegies in the sun?

Charles 'Old Hoss' Radbourn, 1886
(Boston Beaneaters)

Crouched in the back, the official team

portrait, his gesture above a teammate's shoulder:
who is he giving the finger to?

Players, those fielders from New York

maybe, who taunt their league rivals with snorts,
bored with delay in the April

dugouts while waiting to pose for their own team

photo. Or maybe it's Radbourn's
scorn for these 'pictures' that's lifted his digit so

snidely, irate at the tripod and bellows

holding the game from its opening pitch. Or
managers maybe, or press who reported drunken

brawls and philandering.

Maybe it's time with a capital T that faces Radbourn's
finger, a signal he's sent from his age to ours,

showing he knows we're all stuck in a world

made by palookas who dream the fast buck while
playing each other for suckers,

so why not break the measure this once

just to say Fuck You
and So What, it might be the only

thing that's left worth doing,

the only thing we're any good for
in this unexamined life.

Fruit Fly

So slight, no weight, a non-bug,
it wafts past
like an ash flake bobs
above a bonfire's heat,
its shape
an ephemeral asterisk.

Do fruit flies ever die of old age?
At what moment are they living
and then they're dead?
The only times I've seen them die
were flat between hands,

or dialing out their limits of energy
in a glass of stale beer.

When Voyager 1
was scheduled to clear
the solar system,
NASA signalled its onboard camera
to swing back
and take a picture of home. Six
billion kilometres out,
Earth's photo
a 'pale blue dot' .12
pixels in size.
I am in there too,
a child in trampled clover.

If I stand on a scale
and hold the fruit fly in my hand,
does the needle drop a bit
the second it dies?

Where once there was nothing, something.
Where once there was nothing, nothing.

Close All Tabs

I've been reading how they still dredge up
        tacks and ivory eyelets
scattered near Simon the Cobbler's shop,
        where Socrates

often stopped to chinwag in the Athenian agora.
        As the weather clears
and the austere linden sags into leaf, I watch
        our neighbours

empty out their rooms across the street,
        propping odds, ends and bags
of garbage against the realtor's sign; a big, bold SOLD
        in red Calibri.

Of the agora scrap, the ancient inventory
        piles up: amphorae,
broken capitals and *ostraka* used as votes to exile
        fellow citizens,

so many loops and lines alike the same hand
        must have carved them,
proof of ancient vote-rigging. We think the news is over,
        but it never is.

Mid-May I watch and rewatch the Madsen doc
        on Onkalo, the 'hiding place'
in northern Finland. Did I mention you should see it?
        At surface the clocks

run very fast, Peter Wikberg notes in his Scandinavian
              accent, *while in the rock*
it goes very, very slowly. His subject is the shelf life
              of nuclear waste,

where they hope to stash it away forever.
              Greek diggers raised
curse tablets found in ancient wells. Socrates might
              have known their authors:

students, merchants and neighbours who shared a bench
              in the Theatre of Dionysus
and heard the rhapsodes stitch Homeric tales into local
              stories of their own,

the orange Attic sun radiant on the southern slope
              of the Acropolis. Onkalo
will be closed and backfilled with rows of radiation tubes
              secured in passages

five kilometres below. *Conditions on the ground*
              will change, Berit Lundqvist
admits at the table next to Wikberg. *On the surface you never*
              know what's going to

happen. It could be wars; it could be economic depression.
              A caribou lifts its muzzle
and listens across the taiga's granite and snow. My neighbours shift
              a shovel, rake

and lawn chairs from back shed to scuffed, grey porch
        for moving day, clear
a bookcase of knick-knacks and novels, then clear the wall
        of shelves and art,

posing tiredly in bare windows as I browse
        and click, exploring links.
'I bind Euandros with a leaden bond,' one tablet states,
        the goal to handicap

a rival actor in performance. This curse was scraped
        into hammered lead, rolled
and clasped with tacks, then submerged to set its spell
        in motion. Online

new headlines replace Fukushima and Damascus, the late
        Eurozone undertow
shored up in an Athenian square where a pensioner
        in protest and despair

has blown his brains out. *Sing, goddess, sing the rage*
        of Peleus' son Achilles,
Euandros intones to the festival crowd, his voice
        steady and clear,

the theatre's tiers raised with broken stone from older
        temples. By June,
new neighbours paint the pine railing and steps
        with two fresh coats

of biscuit-brown acrylic. I've watched them watch the street,
      weighing their lives
by what they chose to leave or take, knowing
      we must make

strange with a place before we inherit the sense
      of never having been
anywhere else, and curse it for ruin, and stoop to paint
      the porch again.

We sing to free ourselves from the room
                                    —Wild Flag

Notes and Acknowledgements

'Vicious': *Ethos anthropos daimon*: 'A man's character is his fate.'

'Dance': Osel Hita Torres, the name of the boy chosen by the Dalai Lama as a reincarnation of a spiritual leader, denounced the Buddhist order in his twenties, citing 'the misery of a youth deprived of television, football and girls.' Taken away from his family as a child and forced to live a monastic, secluded life, he had been allowed to socialize only with other reincarnated souls, and by eighteen had never seen couples kiss. At the time of writing, he was studying film in Spain. The epigraph for the poem is his reaction to his first disco experience.

'Circa Now': Michael Madsen, dir., *Into Eternity: A Film for the Future*. (Denmark, 2010); Claudio Magris, *Danube* (London: The Harvill Press, 1999).

'In Event of Moon Disaster': Lawrence 'Titus' Oates was an Antarctic explorer on Scott's ill-fated expedition to be the first to reach the South Pole. Aware his severe frostbite was jeopardizing his companions' survival on the return journey, he famously announced, 'I am just going outside and may be some time,' before exiting their tent into the blizzard. His body has never been found.

'Ten Years': see Virgil, *The Aeneid*. Book 3.

'Loot': Lawrence Rothfield, *The Rape of Mesopotamia*. (Chicago: University of Chicago Press, 2009).

'Talk':
'The intellect of man is forced to choose
Perfection of the life, or of the work ...'
– 'The Choice,' W.B. Yeats

'End Times': This poem borrows images from the article 'Life in the Zone' by Steve Featherstone, published in *Harper's* magazine (June 2011). Lines in italics are borrowed from Svetlana Aleksievich's *Voices from Chernobyl: The Oral History of a Nuclear Disaster*. (New York: Picador, 2006).

'Charles 'Old Hoss' Radbourn's Finger, 1886':
(First known photograph of the middle finger)
Greeks weren't the source of its phallic connections necessarily, though
first to imply an offensive nature,
documents claim. In *The Clouds* by Aristophanes
Socrates lectures on poetic meter. A novice who
stresses he certainly knows what a dactyl
is, then produces his middle digit, since dactylos
signifies both a finger and rhythmic measure, a long and then two
shorterish spans like the joints of
fingers, or a penis and testicles, the last a dactylic word like *poetry*
which has a falling rhythm ...

So many thanks to my family and friends. I am extremely grateful for support provided through the Canada Council for the Arts, the Ontario Arts Council, the City of Ottawa and the Banff Centre Leighton Colony during the writing of this book. Some poems were published previously in *Arc* magazine, *The Walrus*, *The Best Canadian Poetry in English* 2012 and Toronto Poetry Vendors. Thank you to the editors. A version of 'Vicious' was performed as part of the Very Short Play Festival 2011. Much thanks to John Koensgen and New Theatre of Ottawa. Thanks to Alana Wilcox, Leigh Nash and Evan Munday at Coach House; to Harold Hoefle, Simon Armitage and Ken Babstock for comments; and I'm especially grateful to Kevin Connolly and my editor Jeramy Dodds for superb edits.

About the Author

David O'Meara lives in Ottawa, Ontario. He is the author of three collections of poetry, including most recently *Noble Gas, Penny Black* (Brick Books, 2008), and a play, *Disaster*, nominated for four Rideau Awards. His poetry has been shortlisted for the Gerald Lampert Award, the ReLit Award, the Trillium Book Award, a National Magazine Award, and he has won the Archibald Lampman Award twice. He is the director of the Plan 99 Reading Series, Artistic Director of VERSE-Fest (www.versefest.ca) and was the Canadian judge for the 2012 Griffin Poetry Prize.

Typeset in Albertan, which was designed by the late Jim Rimmer of New Westminster, B.C., in 1982. He drew and cut the type in metal at the 16pt size in roman only; it was intended for use only at his Pie Tree Press. He drew the italic in 1985, designing it with a narrow fit and very slight incline, and created a digital version. The family was completed in 2005 when Rimmer redrew the bold weight and called it Albertan Black. The letterforms of this type family have an old-style character, with Rimmer's own calligraphic hand in evidence, especially in the italic.

Printed at the old Coach House on bpNichol Lane in Toronto, Ontario, on Zephyr Antique Laid paper, which was manufactured, acid-free, in Saint-Jérôme, Quebec, from second-growth forests. This book was printed with vegetable-based ink on a 1965 Heidelberg KORD offset litho press. Its pages were folded on a Baumfolder, gathered by hand, bound on a Sulby Auto-Minabinda and trimmed on a Polar single-knife cutter.

Edited by Jeramy Dodds
Designed by Alana Wilcox
Cover design by Eric Schallenberg
Author photo by Rémi Thériault

Coach House Books
80 bpNichol Lane
Toronto ON M5S 3J4
Canada

416 979 2217
800 367 6360

mail@chbooks.com
www.chbooks.com